GUIDE

to

GREATNESS

for

GRADUATES

...and all phases before and after...

3G

Written and Edited by Johnnerlyn Johnson

Guide to Greatness for Graduates...and all phases before and after...3G is by Author Johnnerlyn Johnson.

© 2020 | Johnnerlyn Johnson
ISBN 0578510243, 9780578510248

Johnson Five
Publishing
johnnerlynjohnson1@gmail.com

Contact & Order Information

Johnnerlyn Johnson's contact information is as follows:
Website: http://jjohnsonwrites.weebly.com/
Facebook: https://www.facebook.com/johnnerlyn.johnson
Instagram: https://www.instagram.com/guide_to_greatness_4_graduates/
Twitter: @JohnnerlynJ
YouTube: https://www.youtube.com/user/beseenandnotheard
Email: johnnerlynjohnson1@gmail.com
Mail: Johnnerlyn Johnson | P.O. Box 2260 | Laurinburg, NC 28352

Order *Guide to Greatness* online:

Amazon, Barnes & Noble, Better World Books, Books-a-Million, Ebay, Goodreads, LuLu.com, IndieBound, Walmart

Dedication

3G is a timeless book dedicated to anyone who equates success with trying hard and moving forward. There is no exact formula for success. There may be pitfalls, but the hope is that there will be more peaks than valleys.

There are two reasons that we should look back: to see how far we have come and to reflect on wholesome memories.

If you are ready to harness up, hold on tight, grab success by the reigns, and stop at nothing until you arrive, print and sign below:

_____

Print Name

_____

Sign Name

Class of _____

"Greatness begins inside of you; as it emanates, watch it permeate."

– J. Johnson

Guide

to

Greatness

for

Graduates

...and all phases before and after...
3G

Johnnerlyn Johnson

Table of Contents

Foreword

I met Ms. Johnnerlyn Moore, who later became Mrs. Johnnerlyn Johnson, at Marlboro County High School during the summer of 1999. She was teaching a summer English class, and I had just been hired as the principal.

After writing and procuring a seed grant to revive the school newspaper, rebuilding the Journalism program, and helping to improve the English II Exit Exam scores, Mrs. Johnson later earned a spot into our administrative team. At that time, she, along with a team of 16 teachers and buy-in from various stakeholders, successfully developed a Freshman Academy under the auspices of a Bill & Melinda Gates Smaller Learning Communities Grant.

The commonality that we held 21 years ago, and still hold today, is the knowledge that hard work truly pays off.

Because of her unconquerable work ethic, it has come as no surprise to me that Mrs. Johnson has penned her first book. This is going to be the beginning of many projects for this phenomenal young lady who respects herself, values others, and has been a bright light within the world for the 21 years that I have known her.

As you read and work through *Guide to Greatness*, you will find that this is a workbook with the key word being "work". Remember, hard work pays off.

Mr. Rocky Peterkin,
Assistant Vice-President of College & Career Readiness,
Robeson Community College

Acknowledgements

Guide to Greatness for Graduates: 3G was born as I began writing a letter for my children to address a <u>barrage</u> of life's issues. The letter <u>morphed</u> into an actual book for them to reference throughout their lives, and I began to think more globally of others who could benefit from heartfelt messages and pearls of wisdom.

My mother always gave me the latitude to create and chart my own course. She often said, "Johnya, you should write a book." As a child, I thought, "Write a book about what...?" It was somewhat of a <u>defeatist</u> question, but I want to believe I questioned it with normal doubt because I had not yet experienced situations that would become lessons for me and eventually serve as a source of strength for others.

To that end, I acknowledge my parents, Mrs. Betty Jean Munnerlyn Gilchrist and Mr. Archie Gilchrist, who love me and others unconditionally. I also acknowledge my grandparents, Mr. Daniel and Mrs. Esther Munnerlyn, for their perfect wisdom, love, and guidance. I further acknowledge my supportive husband, David, our children; our siblings; my biological father, the late Mr. Johnny A. Moore; other family; a host of special friends; and the entire village for the constant encouragement.

Special thanks again to my "Mama Betty" who retired as a high school English teacher in 2006. Thanks for having another set of proofreading eyes on *Guide to Greatness for Graduates*.

Introduction

Regardless of the level of education you are completing or have completed, *3G* is intended to be a tool for graduates, students, and/or students of life.

The *Merriam-Webster* definition of the verb form of graduate is <u>multifarious</u>: 1) to pass from one stage of experience, proficiency, or prestige to a usually higher one; 2) to change gradually; the noun form means one who graduates.

The spirit in which this book was written is one that focuses on the positive changes that one sees as he or she progresses from one stage to the next.

If you are in, have been in, or will ever be in one of these categories, *3G* is for you: nursery school, daycare, pre-k, kindergarten, primary, intermediate, elementary, middle school, junior high school, high school, alternative school, home school, private school, community college, four-year college/university, educational specialist, masters, doctorate, <u>juris doctorate</u>, or perhaps you are in the best category of education, and this is the student of life category.

3G is an <u>introspection</u> tool. The reflections at the end of each passage encourage you to think critically because the questions begin with verbs from varying levels of Bloom's Taxonomy. The passages begin with verbs because this is a book of action. Being successful means going after what you are seeking and embodying the definition of a verb. Finally, to help you fine-tune your vocabulary skills, a glossary for you to complete has been included.

Define Your Passion

There are many things you CAN do, but there are some things you were BORN to do. That "thing" that you were born to do is your passion. How do you know what it is? It is that "thing" that you spend the most time doing which is not required of you. When you determine your passion, live it, breathe it, and be it. Your passion can become or most often parallels your gift(s), and your gift(s) create opportunities for you.

When you have truly found your passion, you will not be able to rest until you pursue it.

Reflection: Identify your passion(s). What is it that you cannot stop thinking about? How are you working daily to strengthen those passions?

_____

_____

_____

_____

_____

_____

Live Without Regrets

Ten, twenty, or thirty years from now, you do not want to lament while thinking of the things you wish you would have done. Instead, act on your goals, activate your idea of faith, and believe that you will reach those goals. Les Brown's quote is appropriate here: "The graveyard is the richest place on earth, because it is here that you will find all the hopes and dreams that were never fulfilled, the books that were never written, the songs that were never sung, the inventions that were never shared, the cures that were never discovered, all because someone was too afraid to take that first step, keep with the problem, or determined to carry out their dream."

Reflection: Devise your 30-year plan for success.

_____

_____

_____

_____

_____

_____

Wish No Harm

Never wish harm. If people do wrong, they will get it back.

Throughout life's journey, meeting nice people is <u>inevitable</u>. However, there will be people who will be deceitful, selfish, and full of <u>disdain</u> towards you, and they will think nothing of it.

It is sometimes a kneejerk reaction to say or think, "I hope they get back the same (fill-in-the-blank) that they are dishing out to me." The truth is that they will, so you do not have to wish for it. Some people call it <u>karma</u>, and some believe in a <u>vengeance</u> that is more divine. Regardless, the tables will turn. Just wait on it.

Reflection: Explain how wishing harm on others, or *getting someone back*, can backfire on you.

_____

_____

_____

_____

_____

_____

Exercise and Eat Healthy

As you venture into the world of more responsibility and independence, you will be responsible for your own health, preparing your own meals, and even making your own medical appointments.

You may decide to order pizza late at night, drink delicious coffee drinks for breakfast, and sit in 24-hour restaurants at 2:00 a.m. If you are not careful, your waistline will expand, and your health will decline. Therefore, eat in moderation, drink enough water, and keep moving. Your future body will thank you.

Reflection: Familiarize yourself with the "Freshman 15" concept; then create a realistic health plan.

_____

_____

_____

_____

_____

_____

Envy Not

Never envy what someone else has. One never really knows what others have had to sacrifice, deal with, or have thrust upon them to receive what they have.

Seeing someone with extensive weight loss could be the result of dietary discipline, or it could be the result of a life-threatening illness. That "rich" person's possessions could be solely through hard work, or he/she could have received a settlement due to a tragic loss.

Do not waste moments of your precious time wondering about another person's standing because it has nothing to do with you. Instead, capitalize on your own uniqueness.

Reflection: Generate a list of what you love about yourself.

_____

_____

_____

_____

_____

_____

Treasure After-School Friends

Childhood friends are dear and share many memories with you. However, you will meet some of your greatest friends after school (i.e. during college, the military, work, etc.). The camaraderie of roommates, study buddies, fellow soldiers, team members, etc. is magical because you are developing a "new you" with a "new crew".

If you are college bound, I hope you get a trustworthy roommate. You can be assets for each other to make sure you keep your space in order, dine well, maintain a life balance, attend classes, etc.

Reflection: Devise a list of your friends. Add on as you acquire more. Hopefully, you will not have to unfriend anyone. (LOL!)

_____

_____

_____

_____

_____

_____

Accept Rejection

Rejection is absolutely fine! How would it feel if you got everything your heart desired? Frederick Douglass said, "Where there is no struggle, there is no progress." His quote carries an abundance of merit. Some progress will be effortless, but you will also encounter difficulties.

Remember that not all of your desires will be granted. You will experience some tough hits, yet this process will cause you to grow stronger when you realize that you were denied an opportunity because there was a better one in store. Allow rejection to strengthen you.

Reflection: Tell about a time rejection worked in your favor.

_____

_____

_____

_____

_____

_____

Mind Your Manners

"Having manners and knowing how to treat people will take you places that money will not," is what my mother drilled into the psyche of my siblings and me. Having manners is knowing how to conduct yourself and treat people such as: saying "thank you", "you're welcome", speaking to people, holding the door, and saying "excuse me".

During a scholarship interview, I had to discuss the man for whom the scholarship was named. I knew next to nothing, so I spoke in general terms. When I learned I received the scholarship, the award letter read, in part, "We were disappointed that you did not know much about the namesake of the scholarship, but we were so impressed with your personality, your smile, and your handshakes with each of the panelists that we wish to welcome you to the family and award you the scholarship!"

I found favor with the committee through my manners.

Reflection: Circle the qualities that often describe you.

cheerful	reserved	loyal	extrovert	mean	uptight
fearful	quiet	standoffish	fearless	touchy-feely	diplomatic
dependable	spontaneous	planner	persnickety	confrontational	
tactful	introvert	unbothered	liberal	fair	sentimental
conservative	pre-occupied	impersonal	confident	daring	
judgmental	tacky	ambivert	caring	energetic	

Respect All Professions

I once heard a story of a gentleman who, <u>heretofore</u>, will be known as Mr. C. Mr. C was a school custodian. His co-workers were unaware that Mr. C earned both his undergraduate and graduate degrees. He watched carefully as *some* of his co-workers <u>ostracized</u> him and ignored him as he greeted them each morning, yet he was pleased that there were *some* fellow employees who respected him.

A few school years later, Mr. C became the principal of that school! He said that he would never forget the astonishment on some of the faces of those who mistreated him upon realizing that their new supervisor was once that custodian who they disregarded.

Reflection: State some excuses people make for looking down on others. Then discuss why these excuses are not valid.

_____

_____

_____

_____

_____

_____

Use a Black Pen

My <u>pristine</u> 11th grade U.S. History teacher said, "Baby, you need to write in black ink. It's formal, honey." Considering her advice, when bright colors are used for formal papers, etc., it causes the paper or event to appear less formalized. Much like your attire at a "Black Tie Affair", try to keep your documentation formal as well.

Keeping this memory in mind, and as a college instructor, I do not grade in red ink. To me, it can be psychologically damaging. The first feedback my professor gave me during my freshman year looked like he lost a pint of blood on my paper given the amount of red ink. I was bruised, yet I gained from the feedback. At the same time, I vowed that I would not do that to my students.

Reflection: List some formal documents that you will have to sign.

_____

_____

_____

_____

_____

_____

Use Dictionaries

Look up the definition of words! It does not matter if you use an online version; consult a large, hardback copy; or use one that fits in your pocket.

Language is constantly evolving. Over the past decade, *Merriam-Webster* has added nearly 1,000 new words such as: *side-eye, photobomb, microagression*, etc. (Has 'Run' Run <u>Amok</u>?)

You would be surprised to know the actual meaning, origin of words, and the number of definitions that even a common word has. For example, according to npr.org, the word "run" has 645 definitions! (Has 'Run' Run Amok?)

Reflection: Consult the article, "Has 'Run' Run Amok" to see additional words. (Conduct an internet search to find the article.)

_____

_____

_____

_____

_____

_____

Know About *Know/No*

Know/No are homophone pairs. This is a literary term meaning two or more words having the same pronunciation but different meanings, origins, or spellings.

wretched/ratchet   their/there   to/too/two

  your/you're   hear/here   so/sew

Not only during texting and social media posting, but also during essay writing, their/there/they're and to/too/two are most often confused. It is important to know the correct word usage as you compose documents. There are still <u>grammarians</u> out there whose first impressions of you are formed by your writing.

Reflection: List more homophone pairs or trios.

  sail/sell   ore/oar   aloud/allowed

_____

_____

_____

_____

Craft a Signature

Signatures are written promises or endorsements that you are in agreement with what you wrote, that the check is yours, and/or that you agree with document(s) presented to you.

Learn how to write and read cursive writing. Even if you did not learn cursive in school, teach yourself. Then create a cool signature. The style of your signature, which is typically in cursive writing, says a lot about who you are.

Reflection: Practice writing your signature.

Sample Signatures:

_____

_____

_____

_____

_____

_____

Defy Limitations

Do not become defined by the limitations that anyone puts on you. Historically, entire groups of people have been <u>marginalized</u>. While it may be <u>overtly</u> illegal to limit entire groups of people today, as it has been historically done, <u>covert</u> limitations are still placed on people.

Personally, when someone places limitations and/or low expectations upon me, that is when I strive to work harder to prove to myself that the <u>naysayers</u> are wrong.

Reflection: Tell about a time when you had to work against a limitation that someone placed upon you.

_____

_____

_____

_____

_____

_____

Win In Your Head

Win in your head prior to even engaging in what it is you are trying to achieve. Winners win in their head before they even begin. There's an old adage that says, "The race is not given to the swift, but it is given to the one who thinks he (or she) has already won."

The "self-fulfilling prophecy" carries a great deal of merit as well as the adage "As a man thinks, so is he." These sayings prove that winning has to be in the head and heart of one who tries even before he or she begins.

Reflection: Explain what you think a self-defeating attitude is. How can it be avoided?

_____

_____

_____

_____

_____

_____

Respect Authority

Be respectful of those in authority over you. Respect may not always mean being in agreement, but it is inevitable that everyone will have to answer to someone at some point. Furthermore, greater success is achieved when there is a respect for leadership. Authority figures can be parents, siblings, clergy, bosses, bill collectors, police, and so much more. Obviously, the authority figure should be worthy of respect by carrying himself/herself in an upright manner.

With authority, there are rules. When there are rules, there is order. When there is order, the task at hand can be accomplished.

Reflection: List those that have been, are, or will be in authority over you. Likewise, who are you in authority over?

_____

_____

_____

_____

_____

_____

Follow Your Mind

It is good to be unique; follow your own mind. If you choose to share certain aspects of your life with others, you are inevitably going to hear: "If it was me, I would have said... I would have done..." Perhaps they would have, but their course of action does not have to be imposed upon you.

Do not fall prey to the burden of <u>imposition</u> by others. Trust your own thoughts and decisions. Seeking wise counsel is good, but do not set out to constantly solicit advice from those that do not mean well because you will be a broken-sailed ship that is tossed and driven by the waves of others.

Reflection: Formulate a list of areas in which you most often seek advice. To whom do you turn to for advice?

_____

_____

_____

_____

_____

_____

Feed The Hungry Brain

Continuous learning, "aha" moments, intellectual discussions, reading, and stimulating conversations are surefire methods in which one grows <u>dendrites</u> in the brain.

"The important thing is to be actively involved in areas unfamiliar to you," says Arnold Scheibel, former head of UCLA's Brain Research Institute. "Anything that's intellectually challenging can probably serve as a kind of stimulus for dendritic growth, which means it adds to the <u>computational</u> reserves in your brain." (Golden & Tsiaras 62)

Get out of your comfort zone, and stimulate your brain!

Reflection: List the ways in which you engage mentally that help you feed your brain.

_____

_____

_____

_____

_____

_____

Talk Loudly

Enunciate. Articulate. Speak audibly and clearly enough for people to hear and understand you. Doing so is a sign of confidence.

Think of prospective employers. If they are greeted with ineffective communication, they are not going to be impressed. On the other hand, a prospective employee who shakes hands, speaks with a robust voice, and exudes confidence is the one who will grab the employers' attention because they equate speaking effectively with confidence. Confidence is what go-getters have, and go-getters will help move the organization forward.

Reflection: Determine other qualities that potential employers seek in job candidates.

_____

_____

_____

_____

_____

_____

Give Firm Handshakes

People will respect you more after being greeted or bid farewell with a firm handshake. A tight grip during a handshake, just like speaking audibly, equates with confidence.

William Chaplin, an associate professor of psychology, found, "Those with a firm handshake were more extroverted, open to new experiences, less neurotic and shy than those with a less firm handshake." ("Your Handshake...You Think")

Furthermore, "...there is a substantial relation between the features that characterize a firm handshake (strength, vigor, duration, eye contact, and completeness of grip) and a favorable first impression."

Reflection: List other ways to make a positive first impression.

_____

_____

_____

_____

_____

_____

Don't Wear Cheap Shoes

On Mother's Day 2015, I went to urgent care because I was experiencing severe foot pains. After the x-rays, Plantar Fasciitis is what the doctor suggested; however, he did not actually make a diagnosis. He prescribed some <u>OTC</u> ibuprofen, and the next bit of advice the doctor told me was, "Wear some good shoes." He said, "It took me just a few days of walking on this hard emergency room floor [as an ER doctor] to realize that I must invest in good shoes."

Reflection: Rate the level in which you invest in your total self (i.e. mental/physical health, appearance, socialization, etc.). Should it be more or less?

_____

_____

_____

_____

_____

_____

Look Me In My Eyes

Nothing says confidence like being able to look someone directly in his or her eyes when speaking to them. There are some people who are hired as body language experts, and their chief responsibility is to determine what people are saying through their movements, posture, facial expressions, and other nonverbal forms of communication. They observe: eye contact, fidgeting, crossed arms, etc. Looking one in the eyes speaks volumes such as, "I am confident, and I have nothing to hide."

Reflection: Compose some methods to overcome nervousness. What are some situations that may result in you becoming nervous?

_____

_____

_____

_____

_____

_____

Be a Giver

Time, advice, encouragement, a much-needed smile, compassion, directions, tutorial assistance, compliments...

In other words, there are so many ways to give besides giving money. A <u>plethora</u> of people and organizations would welcome your assistance. Research says that those who are givers tend to be happier and have better health.

Reflection: Think of ways in which you have helped, are helping, and will help others.

_____

_____

_____

_____

_____

_____

Recognize The –isms

An –ism is a distinctive practice, system, or philosophy, typically a political ideology or an artistic movement.

Do not buy into any of the negative ones, but be aware of the various –isms that exist such as: ageism, egoism, racism, sexism, elitism, ethical imperialism, etc. Be aware that people are impacted by these words, and thousands are still discriminated against because of some of these very terminologies.

Reflection: Discuss ways to avoid falling victim to certain –isms. How can you help others avoid it?

_____

_____

_____

_____

_____

_____

Believe In You

My family and I attended a semi-pro arena football game to see the Cape Fear Heroes in contest. While waiting for the game to begin, I noticed a banner for *ARRAY* Magazine. I looked up the magazine and sent the owner/publisher an email asking if any writers were needed.

The publisher and owner of *ARRAY* sent me an email within a few short hours to set up a meeting to review my writing samples that next week. The belief in myself, my ability to write, the belief in my confidence, the seizing of an opportunity after seeing the banner, and someone else's recognition of those abilities that exist in me resulted in my fulfillment of multiple roles with the magazine. The same can and will happen for you.

Reflection: Explain what you believe that you can do, become, or create.

_____

_____

_____

_____

_____

_____

Save Your Money

Even if it is only ten dollars per paycheck, save your money. Open a savings account that draws the highest interest. Be sure that it is a savings account that you cannot easily access. Conduct research on ways to invest your money, so you can make it grow and work for you. Walking into the local credit union/bank to speak with a representative, talking to a successful business owner, and completing a financial literacy course are proven ways to learn more about the value of money. A very necessary resource is money, and knowing how to invest properly will afford you many opportunities.

Reflection: Describe some ways in which you are managing your money. What are some of your investment plans and strategies?

_____

_____

_____

_____

_____

_____

Abandon Fear

Do not be intimidated by anyone or anything. Natural apprehensions do occur, yet do not allow those anxieties and concerns to cripple you. Be willing to discuss situations that concern you or stifle you so that they do not impede your ability to move forward. Identify insecurities, try to face them head-on, and address them with specific coping mechanisms so nothing will prevent you from reaching your zenith.

Reflection: Identify methods you can use to rid yourself of any phobia.

_____

_____

_____

_____

_____

_____

Judge Judiciously

Do not be judgmental beyond reason. Remember that not everyone was raised like you. Not to say that the way you were raised was any better than anyone else's upbringing, but not every person that you encounter will have <u>tact</u> and <u>decorum</u>, yet everyone has a right to be respected. No one knows what the person that you are meeting for the first time is going through. Being overly judgmental does nothing to assist him or her especially if they need a listening ear or a judgment-free zone.

Reflection: Discuss how making judgments can be detrimental. In what ways can making judgments be helpful?

_____

_____

_____

_____

_____

_____

Check Your Emotions

"Wearing your emotions on your sleeves" is a cliché that has some merit. It means that one should not make it overly visible when certain emotions are felt. Sometimes, that can be difficult considering not every situation in life is predictable.

Mastering emotions is a useful skill because the world is filled with manipulative people who tend to see expressions of emotions, especially anger and sadness, as a weakness. These are the types of people who will make it their agenda to "push your buttons" just to attempt to gain control of you and/or see you go into distress.

Reflection: Explain how you master your emotions.

_____

_____

_____

_____

_____

_____

Remain Ready

You must be prepared. Ironically, the motto of both Girl Scouts and Boy Scouts is the same: "Be prepared." This motto holds true because you never know where your next opportunity will appear before you.

In order to receive it, keep business cards handy, keep your electronic device nearby, and make extra resume' copies. When that once-in-a-lifetime opportunity comes, you must be ready!

Reflection: Evaluate your level of readiness if you were given, on the spot, the opportunity that you have been hoping for. Would you be ready?

_____

_____

_____

_____

_____

_____

Work Hard; It Pays Off

Hard work does pay off, and the merit of having earned something that you worked so hard for is a process that causes you to appreciate it so much more.

Identify your areas of strength, become trained and highly skilled, and pursue them with aggression. More than likely those areas of strength will shape into your career, and that is an area of your life that you want to be most enjoyable. After all, most statisticians agree that over 90,000 hours will be spent at work for the average person.

Reflection: Describe your dream job/career. What training is required?

_____

_____

_____

_____

_____

_____

Be Happy For Others

Being happy for others ushers in more opportunities for you. You have seen those people whose <u>countenance</u> has fallen when you are blessed, and they appear to have been overlooked.

It is a sad thing because sometimes you may feel that you have to disconnect with your happiness, so they will not be sad. Why should you have to do that? Everyone who works hard will be rewarded. Therefore, whether they are happy for you or not, stay focused and keep moving.

Reflection: List some of the happiest moments of your life thus far.

_____

_____

_____

_____

_____

_____

Laugh At Yourself

Not only should you laugh at yourself, but you should also take the time to laugh in general.

Yale University research asserts, "When we smile, the brain releases dopamine, a neurotransmitter that produces feelings of happiness. Interestingly enough, this effect works both ways: the release of dopamine when we feel happy causes us to smile, and the mere act of smiling causes the brain to release dopamine, which in turn makes us feel happy." (McLean 2011)

Laughing at yourself allows you not to take yourself or life too seriously.

Reflection: List some things, people, and/or situations that you consider especially funny.

_____

_____

_____

_____

_____

_____

Have Older Friends

It may seem strange at first, but it is important to have some positive friends that are at least ten or twenty years older than you are. The reason for this is that they have experienced what you have yet to go through.

Having friends your age is a given, but it is highly likely that you will be able to learn from the shortcomings and successes of older friends simply because they've lived a bit longer.

Seasoned friends can be masterful motivators, they are quick to admit their imperfections, and they are typically genuine and seek opportunities to cheer you on, encourage you, and motivate you. Older friends tend to reel you back in when you may have the notion to behave outlandishly.

Reflection: Justify some situations in which you could use the advice of someone who is at least a decade or more older than you are.

_____

_____

_____

_____

_____

_____

Give Up

Why would "give up" be deemed as advice? The answer is simple: abandon those things that weigh you down, hold you back, and/or prevent you from prospering. In other words, some things have to be given up in order to move one's life forward.

The same goes with individuals. There is an old saying that goes, "Some people come into your life for a minute, some for a season, and some for a lifetime." Give up on keeping someone for a lifetime if he or she was meant only for a minute.

Reflection: Tell about some situations in which you had to give up.

_____

_____

_____

_____

_____

_____

Acknowledge Others

You did not make it to your respective destination by yourself. Always show gratitude for those who served as guardian angels in your path. Obviously family members and encouraging friends serve as examples of guardian angels, but sometimes strangers can act as angels as well.

One never knows when a stranger could become a lifesaver. There are scores of individuals who will have/have had your best interests at heart even if you were unaware.

Whether someone has helped you on purpose or by chance, acknowledge those people by at least thanking them.

Reflection: Create a list of those who helped you along the way. In no way will this list be confined to this space, but it is a springboard.

_____

_____

_____

_____

_____

_____

Take a Break Room Break

When I began taking the courses in my major of Secondary English Education, a professor said, "Don't go to the teachers' lounge because it's often a cesspool of negative energy. The people that hang around in the teachers' lounge will tell you all about how they've tried this and tried that. They will tell you how unsuccessful it was, and they mostly complain. That is not a positive place for a new teacher to be."

That advice has always resonated with me because I still feel leery about going into any break room, lounge, or workroom for any extended period of time.

Reflection: List some places that you avoid. Why do you avoid them?

_____

_____

_____

_____

_____

_____

Love Your Family

Family. You've got to love them. Literally. "Family" is a term that is broad enough to include various family structures such as: traditional, extended, blended, etc. The family is the first system and organization, and the family unit – you will find – typically will be your best, most genuine source of strength, support, and friendship. Do not take them for granted. Invite your siblings and cousins to spend time with you in whatever direction life takes you. Share new experiences with them, and always show gratitude to those who have cared for you.

Reflection: Diagram your family tree.

You may also check out www.familyecho.com

Overcommit Not

Sometimes it is difficult to say, "No." However, it is necessary to decline participation in various projects because the old adage of "spreading yourself too thin" has physical and mental ramifications to it. Furthermore, overcommitting, even for the best multitasker, tends to lead to barely touching the surface rather than one being able to give his or her all.

If someone or an organization needs something from you that you simply cannot do, there is nothing wrong with diplomatically saying, "No. I am unable to commit at this time."

Reflection: Compose a list of people in which it would be hard to say no to. Would you do it anyway? Explain why or why not.

_____

_____

_____

_____

_____

_____

Give Credit to Your Credentials

Years ago, when I was an assistant principal at my high school alma mater, a father and I were waiting for his son to get to my office. I noticed the father was gazing around. He eventually asked, "Where are your credentials?" I said, "Oh, well, I just decided not to put them on the wall." (The true reason was that I never wanted to seem like I was showboating.) He then said, "You know... If I trust you to do the right thing by my child, how am I supposed to know you are trained to know what to do if I can't see proof hanging on your wall?"

I never thought about that. He was right. A display of credentials shows you are well-trained and qualified to do the job with which you have been entrusted. When you earn that diploma, certificate, degree, license, etc., proudly display it. People are waiting to trust you and your abilities.

Reflection: List your present credentials; predict your future ones.

_____

_____

_____

_____

_____

_____

Monitor and Adjust

Flexibility is literally an elastic virtue. In order to get along in life, one has to be able to check the temperature of the situation and know when to change the routine.

Because there is no perfect situation and few predictable situations, you must remember to quietly observe, determine what is happening (especially before speaking in most cases), develop a strategy, and learn how to maneuver a situation to make it better, calm it down, solve it, etc.

Reflection: Explain how you will maintain your resiliency without compromising who you are as you experience new people and situations.

_____

_____

_____

_____

_____

_____

Write a Letter

During a college visitation reception with my son, the admissions staff asked for a show of hands of the prospective students who have ever written a letter, addressed an envelope, and mailed the letter and envelope. Nearly 50% of the hands went up, and I was proud to say that my son's hand was raised because this necessary skill has seemingly found its way out of grade school curricula.

Reflection: Label the parts of a friendly letter.

Unplug

I know it is an <u>indispensable</u> tool. I get it, yet do not become so engrossed with the phone that you forget to engage in the fleeting art of communication. There are certain times when unplugging is a respectful act. Unplugging lets those around you feel that they have your complete attention – unless they are plugged in themselves.

There is a national movement dedicated to the benefits of unplugging. You may be able to earn a sleeping bag for your cell phone if you take the pledge to unplug. For more information, visit the following website: http://nationaldayofunplugging.com/

Reflection: Identify ways in which modes of technology can be distracting.

_____

_____

_____

_____

_____

_____

Call Your Parents

It is best to visit them, but be sure, at the very least, to call your parents daily. Well, at least text them! Speaking from someone who is honored to be a parent, we need your encouragement and the consolation of knowing that you are okay.

You helped us grow, and you taught us so much. A good parent sacrifices the biggest portion of his or her life supporting their children (as well as others). We are still overgrown children in many aspects trying to find our way in life as well, so do not forget us. We love you.

Reflection: Create a profile of your parents. (i.e. where they attended school, number of siblings, favorite colors, favorite foods, etc.) How much do you really know about them?

_____

_____

_____

_____

_____

_____

Budget

As a follow-up to "Save Your Money", create and try to stick to a budget.

Suppose you earn $7,000.00 per month and bring home $5,000.00. Create a sample monthly budget.

Offering/Charity	_____	Food	_____
Electricity	_____	Gas	_____
Cable	_____	Pet	_____
Vehicle	_____	Internet	_____
Savings	_____	Clothing	_____
Retirement	_____	Investments	_____
Mortgage/Rent	_____	Membership #1	_____
Credit Card #1	_____	Membership #2	_____
Credit Card #2	_____	Other	_____
Insurance	_____	Other	_____
Phone	_____	Other	_____
		Total Expenses	_____

After totaling your expenses, how much will you have left? _____

Take Joy With You

"Though we search the world over to find the beautiful, if we do not take it with us, we will never find it." This quote was posted on a picture that my mom bought at the flea market years ago.

The message is plain. Do not seek happiness from other people, places, or things. Carry your own sense of joy, peace, and beauty because therein is where it lies as opposed to outside sources. You should always be your own happy place.

Reflection: Point out reasons why some people feel that materialistic things drive their happiness. Are these reasons valid?

_____

_____

_____

_____

_____

_____

Don't Be Stupid

It is pretty straightforward. Avoid doing dumb stuff. Think before you make decisions that could change the course of your life forever. Oftentimes, spur-of-the-moment decisions bring about negative consequences. Take a moment to think about the situation before acting. You may risk earning the label of old-fashioned or boring, but that is a small price to pay for keeping your sanity and peace of mind. Do not make assumptions before knowing what is really going on, and do not allow others to make decisions for you or dare you to do something that you will regret forever.

Reflection: Write a note to yourself detailing why you should listen to the voice of reason inside your head.

_____

_____

_____

_____

_____

_____

Find Love

Love is a natural phenomenon, and it can occur when you least expect it. Be ready. Position yourself by protecting your feelings and being open to learning about the other person. Sometimes love will work the first time, but sometimes it does not work until the fourth or even the fifth time! In addition to your feelings, protect your body. Never consent to anything that you will regret, that you know is wrong, or that you feel pressured to do. Never allow yourself to be used or abused. Abuse of any kind (i.e. mental, sexual, physical, etc.) is never okay! Finally, before you find love within another person, you must first find love within YOURSELF!

Reflection: Describe the anatomy of a healthy relationship.

_____

_____

_____

_____

_____

_____

Get Back Up

Missed opportunities, errors, defeats, missteps, setbacks, failures, mistakes, obstacles, setbacks, blunders, disasters, mishaps, calamities, pitfalls, fiascos, misfortunes, discouragements, downfalls, slip ups, impasses, miscalculations, roadblocks, and misfortunes are GOING TO HAPPEN. (Of course, these are synonyms. ☺)

Well, not all of these negative circumstances will happen, but quite a few will slither across your path, and sometimes they come when you least expect them. What really matters is how you respond to them when they arise.

Reflection: Devise some realistic "bounce back" strategies.

_____

_____

_____

_____

_____

_____

Afterword

3G is just the beginning. What are other pieces of advice that you would like to see addressed in the next book?

List your ideas below. I would love to publish your thoughts about the book in general as well as your suggestions for additional advice. Then e-mail your thoughts about the book in general as well as your suggestions for additional advice to: johnnerlynjohnson1@gmail.com

_____

_____

_____

_____

_____

_____

Create Your Own Glossary

A glossary contains terms, parts of speech, and definitions. In accordance with the "Use Your Dictionaries" entry, list the part of speech, and define these words. The first two have been done for you.

emanate (p.3): part of speech (<u>verb</u>) <u>to flow out, issue, or proceed, as from a</u>

<u>source or origin; come forth; originate</u>

permeate (p.3): part of speech (<u>verb</u>) <u>to pass into or through every part of</u>

barrage (p.9): part of speech (_____) _____

_____

morphed (p.9): part of speech (_____) _____

_____

defeatist (p.9): part of speech (_____) _____

_____

multifarious (p.10): part of speech (_____) _____

_____

juris doctorate (p.10): part of speech (_____)_____

_____

introspection (p.10): part of speech (_____)_____

_____

lament (p.12): part of speech (_____)_____

_____

inevitable (p.13): part of speech (_____)_____

_____

disdain (p.13): part of speech (_____)_____

_____

karma (p.13): part of speech (_____)_____

_____

vengeance (p.13): part of speech (_____)_____

_____

camaraderie (p.16) part of speech (_____)_____

_____

acquire (p.16): part of speech (_____)_____

_____

psyche (p.18): part of speech (_____)_____

_____

heretofore (p.19): part of speech (_____)_____

_____

ostracized (p.19): part of speech (_____)_____

_____

pristine (p.20): part of speech (_____)_____

_____

amok (p.21): part of speech (_____)_____

_____

grammarians (p.22): part of speech (_____)_____

_____

marginalized (p.24): part of speech (_____)_____

_____

overtly (p.24): part of speech (_____)_____

_____

covert (p.24): part of speech (_____)_____

_____

naysayers (p.24): part of speech (_____)_____

_____

adage (p.25): part of speech (_____)_____

_____

imposition (p.27): part of speech (_____)_____

_____

dendrites (p.28): part of speech (_____)_____

_____

computational (p.28): part of speech (_____)_____

_____

OTC (p.31): part of speech (_____)_____

_____

zenith (p.37): part of speech (_____)_____

_____

tact (p.38): part of speech (_____)_____

_____

decorum (p.38): part of speech (_____)_____

_____

countenance (p.42): part of speech (_____)_____

_____

ramifications (p.49): part of speech (_____)_____

_____

resiliency (p.51): part of speech (_____)_____

_____

indispensable (p.53): part of speech (_____)_____

_____

Appendix

Reflection: Create a record of where you attended school, etc. Also, try to remember the names of your teachers, supervisors, leaders, etc.

Daycare: _____

_____

_____

Kindergarten: _____

_____

_____

1st grade: _____

_____

_____

2nd grade: _____

_____

_____

3rd grade: _____

_____

_____

4th grade: _____

_____

_____

Appendix

5th grade: _____

_____

_____

6th grade: _____

_____

_____

7th grade: _____

_____

_____

8th grade: _____

_____

_____

9th grade: _____

_____

_____

10th grade: _____

_____

_____

Appendix

11th grade: _____
_____
_____

12th grade: _____
_____
_____

College (list each): _____
_____
_____
_____

Military: _____
_____

Internship(s): _____
_____

Workforce: _____
_____
_____
_____

Works Cited

"A quote by Les Brown." Goodreads. Web. 2 May 2016.

American Psychological Association. "Your Handshake May Provide
     More Information to Others Than You Think". 09 July 2000. Web.
     31 May 2017.

Golden, Daniel. Tsiaras, Alexander. "Building a better brain". Life.
     1994 July. 62.

"Has 'Run' Run Amok? It Has 645 Meanings ... So Far." NPR. NPR,
     30 May 2011. Web. 31 May. 2017.

Johnson, Johnnerlyn. "Greatness begins inside of you; as it emanates, watch it
     permeate." Original quotation. *Guide to Greatness for Graduates.*

McLean, Kaitlin. "Can Laughter be Therapeutic?" Yale Scientific
     Magazine. Yale Scientific Magazine - http://www.yalescientific.org,
     12 May 2011. Web. 31 May 2017.

"New Dictionary Words." Merriam-Webster. Merriam-Webster.
     Web. 31 May 2017.

Stat, Terri Yablonsky. "Be generous: It's a simple way to stay
     healthier." Chicagotribune.com. 06 Aug. 2015. Web. 01 June 2017.

Contact & Order Information

Johnnerlyn Johnson's contact information is as follows:
Website: http://jjohnsonwrites.weebly.com/
Facebook: https://www.facebook.com/johnnerlyn.johnson
Instagram: https://www.instagram.com/guide_to_greatness_4_graduates/
Twitter: @JohnnerlynJ
YouTube: https://www.youtube.com/user/beseenandnotheard
Email: johnnerlynjohnson1@gmail.com
Mail: Johnnerlyn Johnson | P.O. Box 2260 | Laurinburg, NC 28352

Order *Guide to Greatness* online:

Amazon, Barnes & Noble, Better World Books, Books-a-Million, Ebay, Goodreads, LuLu.com, IndieBound, Walmart

*Thank you for your support and
for choosing to be great!*

www.ingramcontent.com/pod-product-compliance
Lightning Source LLC
Chambersburg PA
CBHW021221020426
42331CB00003B/410